FOOD & WINE

FOOD & WINE

PAIRING MADE SIMPLE

MARY DOWEY

RYLAND
PETERS
& SMALL

LONDON NEW YORK

For Bob, the chief taster.

First published in the United States in 2002
by Ryland Peters & Small, Inc.
519 Broadway
5th Floor
New York NY 10012

www.rylandpeters.com

10 9 8 7 6 5 4 3 2 1

Library of Congress Cataloging-in-Publication Data

Dowey, Mary.

   Food & wine pairing made simple / by Mary Dowey.
   p. cm.
   Includes index.
   ISBN 1-84172-345-2
   1. Cookery. 2. Wine and wine making. I. Title.

TX714 .D688 2002
641.2'2--dc21   2002066756

All wines listed within are available in
the United States. If you are unable
to find them at your local liquor store,
try the Internet. Below are several
popular sites, but by no means
all of them:

BEVERAGES & MORE
www.bevmo.com

BOTTLE KING
www.bottleking.com

EVINEYARD
www.wines.com

SHERRY-LEHMANN
www.sherry-lehmann.com

WINE LIBRARY
www.winelibrary.com

Editor
Miriam Hyslop
Production
Tamsin Curwood
Art Director
Gabriella Le Grazie
Publishing Director
Alison Starling

CONTENTS

INTRODUCTION

Is matching food and wine really worth the effort? Absolutely! Cleverly paired, even the simplest dish and the humblest wine can both taste terrific, creating a thrilling alchemy of flavors. The opposite, alas, is also true. Choose the wrong wine—one that just doesn't suit the food—and both will taste disappointing. The trouble is that the magic formula for rewarding combinations can sometimes seem frustratingly elusive. With all the different flavors in contemporary cooking, all the different grapes and styles shaping today's wines, how can you feel confident about getting it right every time?

This is a book of straightforward solutions. The basic principles for successful matching are explained simply. The main text is then arranged according to food type, with a wide variety of dishes and wine suggestions under each heading. No matter what you're planning to eat, you will quickly discover which bottles are the best bets for a food lovers' feast.

At the back, there's a list of The Most Flexible Food Wines—especially useful for buffet meals or restaurant outings. A Top 20 Sensational Matches for food and wine is included to set tastebuds tingling, and for those situations where you have an interesting bottle of wine and wonder what on earth to serve with it, there is also an A–Z of the more unusual grape varieties and wine styles, with food recommendations for each.

More than anything else, I hope that you will be encouraged to play around with different flavor combinations. Keep an open mind, be adventurous, and, above all, trust your own tastebuds! Matching food and wine successfully shouldn't be regarded as a baffling new science, but an intriguing process where all the experiments are fun.

It's all too easy to get bogged down in scientific theory about taste components—sweetness, saltiness, acidity, tannin, and so on. Don't! To start with, just think about two key principles: matching weight and flavor.

WEIGHT

Light wines go with light foods; heavier wines with heavier foods. A delicate fish like trout, cooked simply, tastes perfect with a crisp, light white wine (such as Sauvignon Blanc), whereas a meatier fish like turbot is better with a rich, buttery white (such as oaked Chardonnay). The more substantial a dish, the greater your need for a substantial wine. Think about peppered steak, for example. It would swamp a light red, so you'll need to find a pretty powerful one (like a beefy, peppery Australian Shiraz).

FLAVOR

As that last example shows, you can fine-tune your wine choice by echoing the most dominant flavors in a dish. Sometimes those flavors will come as much from the method of cooking as from the main ingredient. For example, pork cooked with apples goes well with a full-flavored, fruity white wine (Vouvray or Semillon)—but pork cooked in a rich tomato sauce with herbs calls for a gutsy, herb-scented red (from the south of France, perhaps).

Here are just a few more examples of flavor-matching to set you thinking. With fish or seafood, fresh, citrussy white wines like Soave or Australian Riesling work in much the same way as a squeeze of lemon. New Zealand Sauvignon Blanc tends to smell of asparagus—so guess what to serve with that! Mature red wines, from Burgundy and northern Italy especially, often have wonderful mushroom and truffle aromas which make them taste exquisite with those ingredients.

Get into the habit of sniffing and carefully tasting every wine that you come across. Think about its flavors and which foods it might suit, and you'll soon be on your way to making great matches of your own.

REGIONAL CLUES

Wines from a particular region often go really well with dishes from that region. For example, grassy young Loire goat cheese and herbaceous Loire Sauvignon Blanc are made for each other. Light Italian red wines taste perfect with most pizza and pasta dishes. Nothing seems quite as delicious with paella as a well-chilled Spanish rosé.

OPPOSITES ATTRACT

Show off your finest wine against a backdrop of very simple food. With elaborate food, do the opposite.

TRICKY FOODS

Although it is possible to enjoy wine with most foods, some are more wine-friendly than others. The troublesome ones can be divided into two groups—the difficult and the downright dangerous.

SOUPS

I never serve wine with soup: it seems senseless—or at least unsatisfactory—to serve one liquid as an accompaniment to another. Not everybody takes such an extreme view, however. If you'd like to have wine, choose a light, dry white—perhaps an unoaked Chardonnay, a Rueda from Spain, or a vegetable-friendly Alsace Pinot Blanc. If the soup is dominated by one particular ingredient—e.g. asparagus, mushrooms, seafood, chicken—look under that heading in the appropriate section.

EGG DISHES

Eggs aren't disastrous with wine. They're just not very good, especially if runny yolk is involved, because it has an annoying habit of coating the tongue and deadening the tastebuds. Sparkling wine or champagne is the best way to cut through it. (What a handy excuse for a ritzy brunch!) ▸ SEE EGG DISHES, PAGE 27.

ICE CREAMS AND SORBETS

Sorbets taste better without wine. Ice cream is a bit problematic; its creaminess gives it some of the same palate-muffling properties as egg yolks, while its temperature numbs tastebuds. ▸ SEE DESSERTS, PAGE 55.

SPICY FOODS

It's often claimed that beer goes better than wine with spicy foods—especially hot, chili-charged dishes. The good news for wine lovers is that some wines can take the heat very well, but you need to choose carefully. ▸ SEE ETHNIC FOODS, PAGE 13.

BLUE CHEESE

While some blue cheeses marry happily with certain wines the most pungent blues may be difficult to match. Fans of Danish Blue and Bleu d'Auvergne, beware! ▸ SEE CHEESE COURSE, PAGE 50.

CHOCOLATE

Although it overpowers many of the lighter sweet white wines, dark chocolate can taste dangerously good with sweet red wines. ▸ SEE DESSERTS, PAGE 55.

DANGER ZONE

VINEGAR

Vinegar makes wine vinegary. That means that pickles, chutneys, mustard, ketchup, mint sauce, vinaigrette dressing are all foods to ration if you want your wine to taste its best. Malt vinegar is the worst offender. Wine vinegar is kinder, balsamic better still, and sherry vinegar the gentlest of all for vinaigrette dressing.

HORSERADISH OR WASABI

Wine-killers, unless used in the most judicious quantities.

CRANBERRY SAUCE

A minor accompaniment, perhaps, but it strips wines of their fruit.

PEANUTS

While peanut sauces get by with fruity wines, peanuts on their own wreak havoc with wine flavors. Choose different nuts or nibbles.

There's no reason why you shouldn't enjoy wine with any of the ethnic foods that are more commonly enjoyed with beer. It's just a matter of picking the right bottle. Subtle wines can be easily swamped by the flavor assault of chilies, ginger, spices, fresh coriander, lemon grass, and other pungent ingredients. You'll need to choose something with plenty of ripe fruit and perhaps a little more sweetness than you might normally favour—otherwise your wine will taste surprisingly lean and mean. On the whole, white wines work better than red, and New World wines are more fusion-friendly than those from Europe.

If you're sharing a number of different dishes, as may well be the case, it's important to pick flexible wines which will suit a wide range of flavors (▶ SEE THE MOST FLEXIBLE FOOD WINES AND RESTAURANT SAFE BETS, PAGES 56–7). Appropriate wines for specific dishes also appear throughout the book. Here are a few general pointers:

CHINESE
Sparkling wine or champagne (it needn't be fancy) suits many mild-to-medium Chinese dishes, cutting through their tongue-coating sauces. Fruity white wines like North American Riesling or Viognier also suit mild or sweet and sour dishes. With meat and stronger spices, fruity reds such as Beaujolais or New World Pinot Noir taste better.

THAI
Here, white wines are definitely more successful than reds. Although Sauvignon Blanc is often recommended, Sauvignon-Semillon and Semillon-Chardonnay blends—with extra fruit and breadth—work better.

INDIAN
Mild dishes go well with fruity white wines, but the hotter the spice, the better off you'll be with a ripe, fruity red such as a Californian Merlot or Zinfandel.

MEXICAN
With light starters like guacamole, try a fruity Chilean Sauvignon Blanc. Meatier, spicier dishes like chili con carne or beef burritos call for a jammy red like Zinfandel, Shiraz, or that Californian speciality, Petite Sirah.

FIZZ WITH FOOD

There's nothing quite like a glass of bubbly to raise spirits, sharpen appetites, and create a giddy sense of occasion. So don't limit your enjoyment of one of the world's most exquisite drinks to birthdays and christenings! Champagne or good sparkling wine makes a lovely aperitif. Serve it with tasty canapés, and you'll ensure that any meal gets off to a stylish, animated start, with conversation flowing as effortlessly as the fizz itself.

Bubbles can also be enjoyed with more substantial things than nibbles—a point that's often overlooked. We've a lot to learn from the Champenois, who take delight in serving champagnes of different styles all the way through a meal. Pop the cork on gastronomic pleasure by trying some of these combinations:

CAVIAR
What luxury! You'll need a rich, full-bodied champagne.

OYSTERS
A light, zesty Blanc de Blancs champagne or domestic sparkling wine— far more sybaritic than a squeeze of lemon.

SMOKED SALMON
Airlines have done their best to devalue the partnership— but good smoked salmon really does taste superb with good champagne.

TAPAS
Cava, Spain's sparkling speciality, is more fun than still wine—and just as traditional.

SUSHI
Any respectable champagne or domestic sparkling wine, but wasabi is dangerous (▸ SEE TRICKY FOODS, PAGE 10).

PROSCUITTO
Looks pretty and tastes pretty fantastic with dry rosé champagne or sparkling wine.

CHEESE PUFFS, CHEESE BISCUITS
Visit the Champagne region, guzzle these at every reception, and you'll see they're made for it!

BRUNCH FOODS
Scrambled eggs, eggs Benedict... Champagne or top-quality domestic sparkling wine turns them into a treat— in bed, especially.

SOUFFLES
A feast of froth... Savory soufflés go well with champagne brut or sparkling wine; sweet ones with champagne demi-sec, or sweet sparklers.

CHINESE DIM SUM
Fizz reduces the tongue-coating qualities of these little dumplings, and other mild Chinese dishes. It needn't be posh though.

THAI STARTERS
Good sparklers from Australia, New Zealand, and California win out.

STRAWBERRIES, OTHER RED FRUITS
Champagne demi-sec and its domestic equivalents —or rosé, which steals the beauty prize.

MERINGUES, ICE CREAMS
Marvellous with sweet fizz— sparkling Vouvray, Moscato d'Asti, or champagne doux.

LITTLE SNACKS

Delicious nibbles with the perfect drink to match may be just what's needed to get a special lunch or dinner off to a good start. But some of these little snacks also work as a first course—or perhaps the only course if you're in the mood for light food and don't feel much like cooking. All the more reason to have a tempting glass in hand…

OLIVES AND SALTED ALMONDS

The most bracingly delicious partner is a well-chilled manzanilla sherry—but a crisp Spanish white from Rueda or Penedès goes well, too. Otherwise, settle for a simple Chilean Sauvignon Blanc.

TAPAS

Something Spanish please! Consider fino or manzanilla sherry, bubbly Spanish Cava, any dry rosé, or one of the crisp whites ▶ SEE OLIVES, ABOVE.

CRUDITES

Plenty of possibilities. Alsace Pinot Blanc is especially good; but you'll manage well with Pinot Grigio, light, unoaked Chardonnay, or Sauvignon Blanc from almost anywhere.

BLINI WITH CAVIAR OR LUMPFISH ROE

▶ SEE FIZZ WITH FOOD, PAGE 15.

TAPENADE OR ANCHOVY TOASTS

The tastes of Provence… Stay in the south of France if you can. A white or rosé Vin de Pays d'Oc or Côtes du Rhône would be terrific. Alternatively, any dry rosé.

GUACAMOLE

Sauvignon Blanc from Chile, New Zealand, or the south of France works best with the coriander and lime juice in this avocado dip, while cooling the chilies. Next best: riper Sauvignons from California and Australia.

TOMATO SALSA WITH TORTILLA CHIPS

Sauvignon Blanc again—
▶ SEE GUACAMOLE, ABOVE—but don't spend a fortune. Chili burn annihilates wine's subtlety.

TARAMASALATA

Forget Restina! Greece now has some terrific dry, lemony white wines to suit. (Assyrtiko and Robola are two varietals to look out for.) Italy helps out with Soave and Verdicchio— or try New Zealand or Chilean Sauvignon Blanc.

HUMMUS

The new-wave Greek whites are just right (▶ SEE TARAMASALATA, ABOVE), and any New World Sauvignon Blanc is pretty good— or experiment with a slightly richer white like Roussanne.

CHEESE PUFFS (GOUGERES), CHEESE BISCUITS

▶ SEE FIZZ WITH FOOD, PAGE 15.
If you're not in a bubbly mood, choose an unoaked white Burgundy like Chablis, Mâcon, or their New World Chardonnay equivalents.

SHRIMP GRILLED ON SKEWERS

Unadorned shrimp are accommodating creatures, so there's plenty of scope: Sauvignon Blanc from Chile, California, or New Zealand, Riesling from the Pacific Northwest or Australia, Spanish Albariño…

CHILI SALT SHRIMP

There's nothing to touch Oregon or Washington State Riesling—but you'll get by with any New World Sauvignon Blanc.

SPICY CHICKEN WINGS

These hot little items can be matched with white or red wine—New World for preference ▶ SEE ETHNIC FOODS, PAGE 12. I'd opt for an inexpensive Chilean Chardonnay or Merlot.

PIZZETTE

It can be white or red, but it should be Italian if possible —or the nearest equivalent. Try a crisp white like Frascati or Pinot Grigio; a light red like Valpolicella or a young Chianti; or Barbera from Italy, California, or Australia. Otherwise, Merlot.

CROSTINI

These toasts, spread with chicken liver paté, tomatoes with basil, and so on, can be paired with white or red wine, depending on whether they're the prelude to a meal or a substantial snack.

▶ SEE PIZZETTE, LEFT.

PROSCUITTO, SALAMI

▶ SEE PIZZETTE, LEFT.
Beaujolais and Loire reds like Chinon and Saumur-Champigny are also excellent with cold meats.

MIXED ANTIPASTI

Multipurpose whites in the right idiom include Soave, Verdicchio, and Pinot Grigio; reds are Dolcetto and Barbera. Abandoning Italy, any crisp Sauvignon Blanc or fruity light red (like Beaujolais or Californian or Chilean Pinot Noir) will do fine.

APERITIFS

Some drinks are better appetite-whetters than others. Try…

Champagne or **sparkling wine**

Fino or **manzanilla sherry**
(from a fresh bottle, very well chilled)

Riesling—German, Australian, or New Zealand

Vouvray Sec

Alsace Pinot Blanc

Albariño, Spain's fashionable white wine

Sauvignon Blanc

They're fresh-tasting, healthy, quick to make... and we're all eating more of them. Salads go well with zesty white wines and light, fruity reds—but don't neglect dry rosé, an under-appreciated salad star.

TOMATO SALAD

The honours are divided between dry rosé (ideally Spanish or southern French) and Sauvignon Blanc— either from the Loire (e.g. Sancerre) or any part of the New World.

FENNEL AND MUSHROOM SALAD

Italian whites like Pinot Grigio, Lugana, and Orvieto flatter fennel, but you won't go far wrong with any light, unoaked Chardonnay.

GOAT CHEESE SALAD

Sauvignon Blanc with goat cheese is pure bliss. For young cheese, pick a Loire version like Pouilly-Fumé or Sancerre; if it's more mature or served grilled on little toasts on the salad, turn to New Zealand, California, or the Pacific Northwest.

CAESAR SALAD

Californian Chardonnay is brilliant: lemony, creamy, and assertive, it's perfect with the Parmesan-rich, anchovy-powered dressing. But any moderately oaked Chardonnay will do.

GREEK SALAD

Light, lemony whites complement the tangy flavors. Look out for new-wave Greek whites like Assyrtiko or Robola, Australian Verdelho or Chile's freshest Sauvignon Blanc from Casablanca.

SEAFOOD SALAD

How many crisp dry whites can you think of? Sauvignon Blanc or dry Riesling from the Pacific Northwest or New Zealand, Pinot Grigio, any citrussy, unoaked Chardonnay...

SALADE NICOISE

A well-chilled southern French rosé is perfect, any dry rosé not half bad—or make a meal of it with a gutsy southern French red (like Minervois or Fitou) or a New World Pinot Noir.

PEAR, WALNUT, AND WATERCRESS SALAD

Aim for a light, pear-flavored white wine like a Côtes de Gascogne or a North American Pinot Gris. Anything too dry will make the walnuts and watercress taste bitter.

CHICKEN SALAD

WALDORF (APPLES AND WALNUTS)
A touch of sweetness is vital; raw apples make dry wine taste horribly sour. Try German Riesling Kabinett or New World Chenin Blanc.

MANGO
Australian Semillon-Chardonnay blends are superb; any dry Riesling is fine.

SMOKED
Go for a lightly oaked Chardonnay.

WARM SALAD OF DUCK BREAST OR DUCK LIVERS

Soft, fruity reds work best. Try Beaujolais or a light young Pinot Noir—from Burgundy, California, or Chile. Next best: Bordeaux rosé.

WARM SPINACH AND BACON SALAD

Easy! Consider any light white (e.g. unoaked Chardonnay, Sauvignon Blanc, Pinot Grigio, Pinot Blanc) or light, fruity red (Beaujolais, Valpolicella, young Pinot Noir).

VEGETABLE DISHES

We probably don't think of choosing wine to suit vegetables half as often as we should. Vegetables are the new meat! Many have very distinctive, dominant flavors that may vary depending on how they're cooked. Pay them a bit of liquid respect.

ASPARAGUS

WITH VINAIGRETTE
Choose your vinegar with care
(▶ SEE DANGER ZONE, PAGE 10) or
substitute a squeeze of lemon, and
you'll enjoy Sauvignon Blanc (Loire or
the New World), a crisp, inexpensive
white Bordeaux, or any Pinot Gris.

WITH HOLLANDAISE SAUCE OR BUTTER
Highlight the creaminess with a subtle
Chardonnay—a Mâcon-Villages or Rully,
perhaps, if you favour Burgundy;
otherwise look to Chile's Casablanca
Valley, California, or New Zealand.

RISOTTO
▶ SEE RISOTTO, PAGE 30.

TOMATOES

TOMATO SALAD
▶ SEE SALADS, PAGE 21.

OVEN-ROASTED WITH GARLIC
A dry rosé from Spain, the south of
France, or Italy hits the spot. You'd also
get away with a crisp Italian white like
Pinot Grigio or any light Chardonnay.

TOMATO SAUCE
▶ SEE PASTA, PAGE 28.

PIZZA MARGHERITA
▶ SEE PIZZA, PAGE 30.

ONION TART

With this Alsace speciality, nothing
rivals Alsace Pinot Gris or Pinot
Blanc—but you'll also manage
with North American Pinot Gris,
Sauvignon Blanc or Fumé
Blanc, or a light Chardonnay.

BELL PEPPERS

ROASTED
Pick up on the hint of sweetness with
a white Côtes du Rhône, a Californian
Marsanne, Roussanne or Viognier, or
any fruity New World Sauvignon Blanc.

STUFFED
Any inexpensive, slightly rustic red
—Spanish, Italian, or southern
French—or be happy with Californian
Syrah or Chilean Merlot.

PEA RISOTTO
▶ SEE RISOTTO, PAGE 30.

LEEK TART
▶ SEE ONION TART, LEFT.

FENNEL, BAKED, OR CHAR-GRILLED

The aniseed flavor of fennel makes
wine matchers tear their hair out—
when they could just lap up a Loire
Sauvignon Blanc (like Sancerre or
Pouilly-Fumé), or one from North
America or New Zealand.

SPINACH

Whether it's used in eggs Florentine, pasta with ricotta, pancakes, or filo pies, cooked spinach makes most red wines taste metallic. Stick to crisp, dry whites—Frascati, Soave, or Pinot Grigio from Italy, or any light Chardonnay.

ZUCCHINI

Bland on their own, they take on personality when cooked with tomato sauce. Choose inexpensive Sauvignon Blanc (Chile, California, Rueda in Spain), or a light red like Valpolicella or Barbera.

GLOBE ARTICHOKES

New Zealand Sauvignon Blanc is the clear winner. Next come all other Sauvignons and crisp Chardonnays. Reds taste dreadful.

EGGPLANT

Stuffed and baked, or cooked with spices, eggplant becomes the meatiest of vegetables. Treat it to a gutsy red like Corbières or Saint-Chinian from the Languedoc, southern Italy's Salice Salentino, Australian Shiraz-Cabernet, or Californian Syrah or Zinfandel.

COUSCOUS WITH SPICY VEGETABLES

A Moroccan red would be authentic, but one from Greece or Lebanon may be easier to find. Otherwise, any New World Merlot.

ROASTED MEDITERRANEAN VEGETABLES

Cooked together, zucchini, eggplant, bell peppers, and garlic go with fruity whites (Côtes du Rhône or Languedoc blends, Californian Fumé Blanc, Australian Verdelho) or light, juicy reds (Beaujolais, inexpensive New World Pinot Noir).

SPICY BEAN CASSEROLE

This calls for a big-hearted red with supple tannins—like Australian Shiraz, Californian Zinfandel, or Italian Primitivo.

BOSTON BAKED BEANS

▸ SEE SPICY BEAN CASSEROLE, ABOVE, or be a bit more off-beat with a Californian Nebbiolo.

ROASTED WINTER VEGETABLES

Carrots, onions, and turnips, slightly caramelized, suit a southern French white which will include grapes like Marsanne, Roussanne, or Viognier. Marsanne, or Viognier from California or Chile will do just as well.

MUSHROOMS

STUFFED AND BAKED

As a first course, try a crisp white Burgundy like Chablis or any unoaked Chardonnay. As a main course, wheel out a not-too-tannic red— Beaujolais, Chilean, or Californian Merlot. An Oregon or Californian Pinot Noir would also be lovely.

RISOTTO

▸ SEE RISOTTO, PAGE 30.

WILD MUSHROOMS AND TRUFFLES

Swank it up with a good Barolo, Barbaresco, or one of the famous, full-bodied Italian wines known as Super Tuscans, or a Californian Sangiovese. With its mushroom and truffle overtones, a mature Pinot Noir—either Burgundy or the best from California— would be just as memorable.

CHEESE DISHES

Wine and cheese are good pals—but they're sometimes choosy about the company they keep. If you're using a cheese with a particularly pronounced flavor, have a look at the Cheese Course section for more specific guidelines.

FONDUE
Purists will hunt out a Swiss white wine—but I'd love an aromatic Alsace Riesling or Sauvignon Blanc from California, Chile, or New Zealand, or a modest white Burgundy like Rully.

SOUFFLES
▶ SEE EGG DISHES, BELOW, OR GOAT CHEESE, RIGHT OR FIZZ WITH FOOD, PAGE 15.

QUICHES
▶ SEE EGG DISHES, BELOW.

PASTA WITH CHEESE SAUCE
▶ SEE PASTA, PAGE 28.

QUESADILLAS
Why not try a jammy red Mexican Petite Sirah? Next best and nearest, geographically, are Sauvignon Blanc or Merlot from Chile or California.

GOAT CHEESE DISHES
Ripe, pungent Sauvignon Blanc from New Zealand, Australia, Chile, or California is a winner with baked goat cheese.
▶ SEE SALADS, PAGE 21, for raw cheese. Goat cheese soufflé is a treat with dry Vouvray.

BLUE CHEESE DISHES
Tricky. Strong blue cheese can strangle dry wine. Try soft, fruity reds like Beaujolais and Côtes du Rhône with gentle blues; luscious Zinfandel with more powerful ones. Barbera suits pizzas.

EGG DISHES

Wine and eggs aren't the best of friends. Runny egg yolk is inclined to coat the tongue, making it difficult to taste wine—and even when it doesn't, flavors often clash. Save your best bottles for something else.

OMELETS, TORTILLAS, FRITTATA
Light flavors (herbs, cheese, potatoes) go best with Pinot Blanc, unoaked Chardonnay, or Spanish whites from Rueda. Bigger flavors (ham, tomatoes cooked with basil, mushrooms) are better with light-to-medium-bodied red wines like Côtes du Rhône or New World Pinot Noir.

SCRAMBLED EGGS
Sparkling wines prevent the tongue-coating effect of runny eggs ▶ SEE FIZZ WITH FOOD, PAGE 15. Otherwise, settle for a Chardonnay—unoaked unless you're having smoked salmon with your eggs, in which case choose a moderately oaked version. Californian Chardonnay works really well.

QUICHES
Try Pinot Blanc or Pinot Gris, any crisp Chardonnay, or a light red like Beaujolais.

SOUFFLES
Match froth with froth ▶ SEE FIZZ WITH FOOD, PAGE 15. If you can't manage that, stick to a middle-of-the road Chardonnay—a Saint-Véran or Mâcon-Villages from Burgundy, maybe, or a subtle Californian version. Goat cheese soufflés have special needs ▶ SEE CHEESE DISHES, ABOVE.

EGGS FLORENTINE
▶ SEE VEGETABLE DISHES, PAGE 24.

PASTA

With a simple, everyday dish like pasta, why not have a simple, everyday wine? Italian whites and reds are the natural choice—especially as Italy now offers so many exciting, well-priced wines. Those made elsewhere using Italian grape varieties—Sangiovese, Barbera and so on—also feel comfortingly authentic. But there are other possibilities.

VEGETABLE-BASED

SPINACH AND RICOTTA

▸ SEE VEGETABLE DISHES, PAGE 24.

PESTO

Whites work better than reds. Choose something like Lugana, Vernacchia di San Gimignano, or Soave from Italy, Alsace Pinot Blanc or unoaked New World Chardonnay.

FRESH TOMATOES AND BASIL

Fresh Italian whites such as Pinot Grigio or Lugana are excellent—but so is any relatively crisp Sauvignon Blanc.

TOMATO SAUCE

You'd get by with a white wine like Pinot Grigio, but reds make a happier marriage. Maybe a young Chianti (or Californian Sangiovese); Barbera from Italy, California, or Australia; or a sunbaked southern Italian like Primitivo and its American "cousin", Zinfandel.

MUSHROOMS

Take your pick between crisp white and round red. In the white camp, Frascati, Orvieto, and unoaked Chardonnay. In the red, Dolcetto d'Alba, Chilean Merlot, and New World Pinot Noir.

SAGE BUTTER

The strong flavor of sage tastes just right with a restrained, cool-climate Sauvignon Blanc—one that's pungent and grassy, not laden with tropical fruit. Try a North-Eastern Italian version for authenticity, or a Sancerre or Pouilly-Fumé from the Loire.

CREAMY

CARBONARA

Counter the richness of eggs, cream, ham, and Parmesan with a fairly crisp white wine. Northern Italians like Pinot Grigio and Gavi perform well, as does Sardinian Vermentino or any light Chardonnay.

CHEESE

Whether it's pasta with four cheeses or macaroni and cheese, you'll need the same crisp whites as for Carbonara—unless you prefer a light red like a simple young Chianti from Tuscany, or Barbera from northern Italy or California.

MEAT AND FISH

MEAT SAUCE (BOLOGNESE)

Red, for sure, and middleweight. Perhaps Chianti Classico or any Sangiovese; Valpolicella Ripasso or a New World Merlot.

SPICY SAUSAGES

Those big flavors cry out for a rich red with plenty of ripeness to cope with the heat. Consider Californian Syrah, Australian Grenache-Shiraz blends, Zinfandel from Chile or California, or anything from Italy's deep south (such as Salice Salentino).

SEAFOOD (CLAMS, MUSSELS, CRAB)

Stick with the Italian "Vs"—Verdicchio, Vernaccia di San Gimignano, or Sardinia's Vermentino. Otherwise, the crispest, driest white you can find. A light Chardonnay would do.

SALMON OR SMOKED SALMON

Chardonnay, unoaked or lightly oaked (Burgundy, northern Italy, Chile, California, New Zealand) is pretty unbeatable.

ANCHOVIES, OLIVES, AND CAPERS (PUTTANESCA)

Not for wimps, this. Go for the contrast of a cooling, neutral white like Frascati or Pinot Grigio, or fight back with a fruity, characterful red—one from Sicily, perhaps, a young Primitivo, or a not-too-full-bodied Californian or Chilean Zinfandel.

PIZZA

Like pasta, pizza begs for a modest wine that reinforces its Italian character—or at least one that's similar in style to the leading contenders from Italy.

TOMATO AND CHEESE (MARGHERITA)
Try a fresh white like Pinot Grigio (great with oregano and other herbs), Soave or a crisp Chardonnay (from Italy or Casablanca in Chile). Lightish reds are fine, too—a decent Valpolicella, perhaps, or Barbera (Italian or Californian).

SEAFOOD
▸ SEE PASTA, PAGE 28.

ANCHOVIES, OLIVES, GARLIC, CHILIES
A dry rosé (southern French, Spanish, Australian) is bang on. If you'd prefer red, choose a Sicilian or Sardinian, head to Chile or California for Zinfandel, or pick a Californian Sangiovese.

SMOKED CHICKEN
Chardonnay rules here. It can be unoaked if you like, but a hint of oak will reinforce that smokiness. Look to Burgundy, Chile, California, or New Zealand.

HAM, BACON, OR SALAMI
No agonizing required. Any light to medium-bodied red is fine. That means Chianti (or any Sangiovese), a northern Italian like Dolcetto, Valpolicella, or Barbera, or any unpretentious Merlot.

SPICY SAUSAGE
▸ SEE PASTA, PAGE 28. The same swashbuckling reds suit.

RISOTTO AND OTHER RICE DISHES

Conveniently, risotto has much the same requirements as its well travelled sister foods, pasta and pizza. *Buon appetito!*

RISOTTO

BASIC
The simplest risotto needs a fresh, light white. Try Pinot Grigio, Soave, or an unoaked Chardonnay.

ASPARAGUS
Sauvignon Blanc (Loire, California, New Zealand, Chile) is the winner; Alsace Pinot Blanc a creditable runner-up.

PEA AND/OR ZUCCHINI, WITH HERBS
▸ SEE ASPARAGUS, ABOVE, but with more choice: add to the list Lugana, Vernaccia di San Gimignano and light Chardonnays or Chardonnay-Sauvignon blends.

BUTTERNUT SQUASH OR PUMPKIN
Match the hint of sweetness with full-flavored Verdicchio, white Côtes du Rhône, Californian Marsanne or Viognier.

SEAFOOD
Frascati, light and gentle, goes down a treat. Pinot Grigio, Lugana or any lean, unoaked Chardonnay is next in line.

CHICKEN
Anything mild and well-mannered. Vernaccia di San Gimignano, Orvieto, or unoaked Chardonnay if it's to be white; Dolcetto d'Alba, Chianti, or a Merlot from any corner of the globe if red.

MUSHROOM
Pinot Noir—slightly mature if possible, whether from Burgundy or the New World—has wonderful mushroomy scents. Southern Italian varietal reds like Negroamaro and Nero d'Avola are suitably earthy, too.

TRUFFLE
A real treat, so abandon modesty and produce an Italian treasure like Barolo, Barbaresco, Amarone, or one of the posh reds dubbed Super Tuscans. Or a top Californian or Australian Sangiovese or Nebbiolo.

OTHER RICE DISHES

PAELLA
There's nothing to touch dry rosé—
Spanish for preference, but any will do.

BIRYANI/ PILAU
Mildly spicy, so you'll need an off-
dry white like German Riesling
Kabinett, Côtes de Gascogne, or
Californian Viognier.

RED WINE
Risotto cooked in red wine should be
drunk with red wine. Be guided by the
recipe—but if you cheat slightly by using
a cheaper or lighter wine than the one
recommended, drink something a bit
more swish.

FISH

"White wine with fish, red with meat" is a rule often repeated—and it's not without foundation. But some fish tastes splendid with red wine, and some cooking methods result in gutsy flavors which make red wine the best option. Keep an open mind.

SUSHI
▸ SEE FIZZ WITH FOOD, PAGE 15. Best still wines are German or New World Riesling, or an inexpensive Sauvignon Blanc from California—but wasabi is a wine-killer ▸ SEE TRICKY FOODS, PAGE 10.

CEVICHE
If you're using lime juice, lime-fresh Riesling from the Pacific Northwest is a brilliant choice. With lemon juice, try Sauvignon Blanc from Chile, California, or New Zealand.

SEAFOOD TERRINE
Chablis or any unoaked Burgundy— or a light, lemony Chardonnay from Italy, Chile, or California.

LEMON SOLE
It's delicate in flavor, so don't over-power it. Consider the Chardonnays recommended for Seafood terrine, or light Italians like Bianco di Custoza and Soave Classico.

TROUT
▸ SEE LEMON SOLE, ABOVE. A zesty Sauvignon Blanc from the Loire (such as Sancerre or Pouilly-Fumé), Bordeaux, or California would also be delightful.

COD
ROAST
What you are after is a light white.
▸ SEE LEMON SOLE AND TROUT, ABOVE.

WRAPPED IN PANCETTA
Meatier territory! While gentle whites such as unoaked Chardonnay or Italian Soave or Lugana are fine, bacon-wrapped cod can take a light red like Chinon from the Loire, a young red Burgundy, or a New World Pinot Noir.

TURBOT
Posh fish, so splash out on an extravagant, rich white—a buttery Burgundy like Meursault, a top Californian or New Zealand Chardonnay, or a really good Bordeaux Graves.

SKATE
A delicate Sauvignon Blanc goes better than the light Chardonnay family (though they're OK). Look to Sancerre or Pouilly-Fumé, cool-climate California, or Chile.

SQUID OR CALAMARI
CHAR-GRILLED
Any crisp, refreshing, slightly citrussy white—Muscadet, unoaked white Bordeaux, Soave, or one of the Sauvignons suggested for Skate.
STUFFED OR IN TOMATO SAUCE
More substance! Dry rosé (south of France, Spain, Australia) is terrific.
SZECHUAN STIR-FRIED
Try a soft red like Chilean Merlot or an inexpensive Pinot Noir from the south of France (there are a few!), Chile, or Australia.

MONKFISH
A subtle, creamy Chardonnay (California, New Zealand, or Burgundy: maybe Saint-Véran) is the star choice, especially with beurre blanc. But it's meaty enough to stand up to red, especially if wrapped in ham or bacon.
▸ SEE COD WRAPPED IN PANCETTA, ABOVE.

SALMON

COLD, WITH MAYONNAISE

If it's wild salmon, it deserves a stellar Chardonnay—Puligny-Montrachet or Chablis Premier Cru for Burgundy lovers, or the best from California, Western Australia, or New Zealand. Farmed fish rates a more modest Chardonnay.

WARM, WITH BEURRE BLANC OR HOLLANDAISE

The same, elegant Chardonnays ▶ SEE COLD SALMON, ABOVE.

WARM, BAKED

Again, ▶ SEE COLD SALMON, ABOVE; but a lightish red would be equally good. Try Chinon or Bourgeuil from the Loire, or a young Pinot Noir from anywhere.

PAN-FRIED IN A SPICY CRUST

The spice makes a soft, fruity red the wisest choice. Pinot Noir from California, New Zealand, or Australia tops the list.

SMOKED

Champagne with really good smoked salmon is a treat (▶ SEE FIZZ WITH FOOD, PAGE 15). Next best thing: a quality Californian Chardonnay. The combination of lemon, butteriness, and gentle smoky oak is exactly right. Or talk yourself into a topnotch Chablis.

GRAVLAX

With the element of sweetness, nothing tastes half as sensational as the Chenin Blanc-based Loire white, Vouvray (demi-sec for preference, but dry is fine). New World Chenin is too fruity. German Riesling—Kabinett or Spätlese—is a better alternative.

FISH PIE

Creaminess and a touch of lemon are the keys. You could have any gentle, slightly buttery Chardonnay, but why not try Spanish Albariño or Italian Lugana for a change?

TUNA

TARTARE OR CARPACCIO

Pick a light, zesty white. Sauvignon Blanc from New Zealand, California, or Chile works well, as does New World dry Riesling.

CHAR-GRILLED

Not just meaty but smoky, too. Best with a softish red like Côtes du Rhône, any inexpensive Merlot, or New World Pinot Noir.

SMOKED FISH

Awkward territory. Smoked fish isn't always terribly wine-friendly, but fino sherry often works. Otherwise, try any moderately-oaked Chardonnay, or experiment with the flavor assault of Gewurztraminer.

FISH AND CHIPS

Any crisp white will be absolutely fine. So, Chablis or any unoaked Chardonnay, a simple white Bordeaux or Bergerac, or any light Sauvignon Blanc.

FRITTO MISTO

▶ SEE FISH AND CHIPS, ABOVE—though you might like a fresh-tasting Italian white with Italian fried fish. Frascati, Soave, Vermentino, Pinot Grigio…

SPICY FISH CAKES

Seek out a ripe, fruity white. New World Sauvignon Blanc (including Californian Fumé Blanc) is good—or try luscious Californian Marsanne, Roussanne, or Viognier.

MALAYSIAN FISH CURRY

▶ SEE SPICY FISH CAKES, ABOVE.

SHELLFISH

Think of a huge platter of shellfish, fresh with the tang of the sea, and needing only a squeeze of lemon. The wine clues are there: crisp, citrussy whites go well with most seafood. But, as always, the weight of the dish is important. Shellfish with sweet, rich flesh (like crab and lobster) tastes superb with slightly more full-bodied wines.

OYSTERS

NATURAL
Their lemon and mineral overtones make champagne and Chablis unrivalled classic matches. Citrussy New World dry Riesling is also a smart choice; Muscadet a low-budget alternative.

COOKED
A lightly oaked Chardonnay—but if the oysters are in a champagne sauce, drink champagne!

MUSSELS

IN A WHITE WINE SAUCE
Entre-Deux-Mers from Bordeaux, Muscadet, or any crisp white.

IN A CREAM SAUCE
Extend the creaminess with a light Chardonnay or Italian Lugana.

WITH GARLIC
More oomph required! Try a subtly oaked Chardonnay or a rich white like Roussanne.

CLAMS

BAKED
Sauvignon Blanc from the Loire, California, or Chile picks up the flavor perfectly.

IN SPAGHETTI ALLA VONGOLE
Choose a crisp Italian white like Pinot Grigio, Frascati, or Sardinian Vermentino.

SCALLOPS

PAN-SEARED
Dry Vouvray, dry Riesling, or Austrian Grüner Veltliner —three mouthwatering matches.

IN A CREAMY SAUCE
Lightly oaked Californian Chardonnay or a middleweight white Burgundy like St Véran.

THAI
Any aromatic New World Sauvignon Blanc will perform brilliantly with coriander, lemon grass, and chilies.

CHINESE
Go for a touch more sweetness, with an off-dry Riesling or Pinot Gris.

SHRIMP

IN THE SHELL
Those citrussy whites again… Chablis (or any zesty, unoaked Chardonnay), Albariño from Spain, or a New World dry Riesling.

CHAR-GRILLED
Any New World Sauvignon Blanc—especially if the shrimps are rubbed with salt and chili.

IN TOMATO AND GARLIC SAUCE
A dry rosé, preferably from Spain or the south of France.

THAI GREEN CURRY
Australian Semillon-Sauvignon or ▶ SEE THAI SCALLOPS, LEFT.

CHINESE
Honey-streaked Alsace, German and New World Rieslings echo the sweetness in the sauce.

CRAB

FRESH
Viognier offers sensational synergy—Condrieu if you're feeling extravagant, otherwise Viognier from Chile, California, or the south of France. White Côtes du Rhône or Marsanne—southern French or Californian—is tasty too.

SPICY CRAB CAKES
A Washington State or Oregon dry Riesling, New World Sauvignon Blanc, or Californian Viognier.

LOBSTER
A total extravagance, so the wine may as well be one too!

COLD
Non-vintage champagne, minerally white Burgundy (try Puligny-Montrachet), or a top drawer Chardonnay from California, South Africa, or New Zealand.

HOT-BUTTERED OR SAUCED
Vintage champagne, rich Burgundy, or the New World's butteriest, most serious Chardonnay.

MIXED SEAFOOD

SHELLFISH BISQUE OR SEAFOOD CHOWDER
Pinot Gris, Chardonnay or fino sherry, at a push.
▶ SEE TRICKY FOODS, PAGE 10.

MIXED SEAFOOD PLATTER
Chablis, Loire Sauvignon, Rueda from Spain, Soave from Italy, zippy young Riesling… any crisp, dry white.

PAELLA
A Spanish rosé for authenticity—but any dry rosé will do.

SEAFOOD RISOTTO
▶ SEE RISOTTO AND OTHER RICE DISHES, PAGE 30.

SEAFOOD SALAD
▶ SEE SALADS, PAGE 21.

CHICKEN

More than almost any other food, chicken is a wine chameleon, adapting itself to a huge range of possibilities. As always, think about the main flavors in the recipe you've chosen and try to pick a wine to suit—but above all, be adventurous!

ROAST

Anything you fancy provided it's not too oaky and tannic. Good reds include Pinot Noir and modest young Syrah or Shiraz, but I rather favour whites. A gentle, creamy Chardonnay is fine but Australian Semillon or a Californian Marsanne/ Roussanne blend is much more exciting.

FRIED CHICKEN

▸ SEE ROAST CHICKEN, ABOVE.

GRILLED OR BROILED

IN HERB MARINADE

Pinot Gris (from Alsace, Washington State, or Australia) is an interesting choice, but a lightish Chardonnay, or soft red like Côtes du Rhône, or a New World Pinot Noir would be grand.

IN CREAM SAUCE

▸ SEE CHICKEN IN HERB MARINADE, ABOVE.

RUBBED WITH SPICES

Fruity wines are spice-friendly. Think about Californian Viognier or Marsanne, Cabernet-Shiraz, or Beaujolais.

COQ AU VIN

Even if you cheat on tradition by not cooking the chicken in red Burgundy, you should try to drink it—or a Pinot Noir from California, New Zealand, or Australia.

CASSEROLE WITH TOMATOES AND HERBS

Go Mediterranean with a Languedoc red like Minervois or a Côtes du Rhône. Or try Chilean or Californian Syrah for a change. Australian Shiraz-Cabernet would be fine, too.

STIR-FRY

Choose a round, fruity white like Semillon-Chardonnay from Australia, or any Viognier.

SMOKED CHICKEN

A smoky, oaky Chardonnay from any country of your choice is the answer. Or enjoy an aged Hunter Valley Semillon, which tastes toasty and smoky without recourse to oak. One of Australia's great wine treasures!

SATAY

Spectacular with Australian Semillon-Chardonnay or, better still, Hunter Valley Semillon. But you'd get by very comfortably with any moderately oaked Chardonnay.

FAJITAS WITH SALSA

Mexican food goes down well with ripe Californian or Chilean Sauvignon Blanc or berry-laden Zinfandel—but you might like to try Mexican Petite Sirah.

RISOTTO

▸ SEE RISOTTO AND OTHER RICE DISHES, PAGE 30.

CHINESE CHICKEN NOODLE DISHES

Californian, Australian, or New Zealand sparkling wine works Chinese wonders (▸ SEE FIZZ WITH FOOD, PAGE 15). Fruity Alsace Pinot Blanc, German Riesling Kabinett, and Australian or North American Riesling also suit.

KORMA

Fruity whites again
▸ SEE CHINESE CHICKEN NOODLE DISHES, LEFT. Or you could try Marsanne from California or Australia and Côtes de Gascogne from southwest France.

TANDOORI

And again, those fruity whites under the last three headings! But fruity reds go down well also. Zero in on Beaujolais-Villages, New World Merlot, or Zinfandel.

BIRYANI

▸ SEE RISOTTO AND OTHER RICE DISHES, PAGE 31.

THAI GREEN CURRY

The two shining stars are Australian Semillon-Sauvignon and Alsace Pinot Blanc. Sauvignon Blanc from Chile, California, or New Zealand gets modest applause.

TURKEY, DUCK, AND GOOSE

If you prepare a festive meal with one of these birds, don't be tempted (as people often are) to serve it with your best red Bordeaux, or a posh Cabernet from anywhere else. Tannic wines like these will make your prized poultry taste dry as sawdust. Instead, think in terms of a topnotch red wine with a soft cushion of sweet, concentrated fruit.

TURKEY

ROAST
Best ideas by far are a generous Rhône red like Châteauneuf-du-Pape, Californian Syrah, or Australian Shiraz—especially a smooth, rich one from McLaren Vale. If you favour white, try any good Burgundy (this could be the moment to indulge in a Chablis Premier Cru), or a top New Zealand or Californian Chardonnay.

COLD
Stick to soft, fruity reds like Beaujolais or New World Pinot Noir, or follow the fun Australian route with sparkling Shiraz.

DUCK

ROAST
Uncork the best Pinot Noir you can afford—from Burgundy, California, Oregon, New Zealand, or Australia; it has the right, gamey flavor plus acidity to cut through the fat. Barolo and Barbera do the same.

BREASTS
WITH CARAMELIZED APPLES OR MANGO
Highlight the fruit with a Riesling from Germany, Alsace, or the New World.
RUBBED WITH SOY, GINGER, AND SPICES
Any New World Pinot Noir works a treat.

CONFIT
Exception to prove the rule: a rather tannic red suits this rich, hearty dish. Madiran from Gascony, home of the goose, is spot on. Or try a seriously good red from Priorato in Spain, a Californian Cabernet, or a meaty Australian Barossa Valley Shiraz.

PEKING OR SZECHUAN
These flavorsome Chinese dishes need a soft red wine with upfront fruit—like Beaujolais or a fairly straightforward New World Pinot Noir. Chile's inexpensive Pinots suit Asian food particularly well.

GOOSE

ROAST
▶ SEE ROAST DUCK, LEFT.
But apple sauce or stuffing suggests a rich, appley white like German Riesling Spätlese or Pinot Gris (Alsace or North America).

CASSOULET
Featuring goose or duck (and often goose fat, too) alongside beans, pork, and lamb this heavyweight southern French dish needs a wine with equal brawn. Stay local if you can.
▶ SEE PORK, PAGE 43.

PORK

True to meat tradition, pork is most frequently served with red wine. Fine, except that it's often cooked with fruits—apples, pears, peaches and so on —which make for happier partnerships with white.

ROAST
Delicious with generous red wines—either medium-bodied, fruity ones like the richer Beaujolais crus (Morgon, Moulin à Vent) and New World Pinot Noir, or fuller styles including northern Rhône reds (Crozes-Hermitage, Saint-Joseph), and their New World equivalent, Syrah/Shiraz. For white wine fans, pork roast with juniper is knockout with Alsace Pinot Gris.

WITH APPLES, PEARS, PEACHES
Strike out! White wines with plenty of fruit and acidity are the thing—Vouvray from the Loire, Viognier from anywhere, Australian Semillon, or a Washington State or Oregon dry Riesling.

WITH PRUNES
Vouvray if there's cream in the sauce; if not, choose a red.
▶ SEE ROAST PORK, ABOVE.

CHOPS WITH MUSTARD
Although mustard can be difficult— ▶ SEE TRICKY FOODS, VINEGAR, PAGE 10—you should survive with any lightly oaked Chardonnay, or a red such as Rioja (or a more humble Spanish Tempranillo), or Merlot.

FILLET IN CREAMY MUSHROOM SAUCE
A lightly or moderately oaked Chardonnay (Californian especially) would be spot on – as would Pinot Noir.

CASSEROLE WITH TOMATO SAUCE
Try a herb-scented southern French red like Faugères, Californian Merlot, or an Australian Cabernet-Shiraz.

SPARE RIBS
BARBECUED
Smashing with New World Pinot Noir, South African Pinotage, or Zinfandel from California or Chile.

CHAR SIU
Not easy. Try a dry rosé or an off-dry white like Vouvray or Semillon-Chardonnay.

CASSOULET
Pair this dauntingly substantial dish from south-west France with a big local red like Madiran, Cahors, or Corbières if you can. Otherwise, a swashbuckling Syrah or Shiraz will do.

CHOUCROUTE
Celebrate the national dish of Alsace with that region's Pinot Gris or Riesling—or try a spicy white like Gewurztraminer.

SAUSAGES
WITH LENTILS
You need a hearty, medium-bodied red. Try a Valpolicella Ripasso, a Tempranillo from Navarra, or a New World Merlot.

SPICY
Tuck into a flavorsome Portuguese red from the Douro or Bairrada, a peppery Californian Zinfandel, or an Australian Shiraz.

SATAY
▶ SEE CHICKEN, PAGE 38.

STIR-FRY
▶ SEE CHICKEN, PAGE 38.
Or try a slightly richer white like Californian or southern French Roussanne or Marsanne.

CHINESE SWEET AND SOUR
▶ SEE SPARE RIBS, CHAR SIU, LEFT.

HAM & BACON

Easy does it! Fruity, medium-bodied wines are the answer here. Keep the heavyweights up your sleeve for richer meats.

HAM

BAKED
White wine lovers should enjoy a lightly oaked Chardonnay or Pinot Blanc. Red supporters can play with Beaujolais-Villages, Loire reds like Chinon or Anjou-Villages, Burgundy (try Givry), or New World Pinot Noir.

PASTA WITH HAM, EGGS, AND CREAM (CARBONARA)
▶ SEE PASTA, PAGE 28.

PIZZA WITH HAM, BACON, OR SALAMI
▶ SEE PIZZA, PAGE 30.

AIR-DRIED (SERRANO, PARMA)
Try a refreshing Italian white like Pinot Grigio or Orvieto, unoaked Chardonnay, dry rosé, or that neglected treasure that's so perfect with these hams fino sherry.

WITH MELON OR FIGS
Amplify the fruitiness with Austrian Grüner Veltliner, a Californian Marsanne/Roussanne blend, or Semillon.

LAMB

Simply cooked, lamb is a showcase food—the perfect foil for a plethora of serious red wines from around the world. If you have a special bottle, this may be your chance to show it off.

ROAST

The most famous matches involve top quality red Bordeaux and Rioja Gran Reserva. Both stunning! But, with their hint of mint, Bordeaux's Saint-Emilion, California's Napa Valley Cabernet Sauvignon, and Australia's Coonawarra Cabernet are also delectable.

WITH GARLIC AND ROSEMARY
The swish Italian reds known as the Super Tuscans and top Chianti Classicos perform brilliantly, alongside Rioja. Californian Sangiovese or Cabernet comes next.

WITH GARLIC, ANCHOVIES, AND OLIVES
Choose a vigorous Côtes du Rhône-Villages like Rasteau, a Languedoc red like Corbières, or a Zinfandel.

SHANKS, BRAISED

Anything mentioned so far!

KEBABS, CHAR-GRILLED

If they make you dream of Greek holidays, try soft, spicy Greek Nemea—but any herb-and-pepper-dusted red will do. Vin de Pays d'Oc reds, Chilean Merlot, Californian Syrah, Australian Shiraz…

MOUSSAKA

Definitely deserves Greek Nemea—but I'd settle for a Languedoc red like Minervois, a modest Chianti, or Chilean Cabernet.

MOROCCAN OR TURKISH SPICED

Try an assertive red like Lebanon's famous Chateau Musar, one from Greece (▶ SEE MOUSSAKA, LEFT), or a Californian Syrah would also be fine.

Unless you're cooking with spice, soft and fruity red wines are best left to one side. Beef generally tastes best with firm, dry reds with a bit of tannin—that mouth-drying substance that gives wines body and staying power.

ROAST

▶ SEE ROAST LAMB, PAGE 45—or you can go for something more tannic and full-bodied. Maybe a Spanish gem from Ribera del Duero or Priorato, a good Châteauneuf-du-Pape, or an Australian Barossa or Clare Valley Shiraz? Argentine Malbec is a brilliant bargain alternative.

BRAISED IN RED WINE

Boeuf bourgignonne, the best-known form, demands red Burgundy. But Syrah or Shiraz will do every bit as well.

COLD AND RARE

Move one step in a softer direction than for roast beef—with Côtes du Rhône, Chilean Cabernet Sauvignon, or Californian Merlot.

CARPACCIO AND BRESAOLA

When served as first courses, these Italian versions of beef are fine with a slightly creamy white like Lugana, or an unoaked Chardonnay. But you might decide that a dry rosé or a lightish red like Valpolicella or Barbera tastes better.

STEAK

▶ SEE ROAST BEEF, LEFT—but if it's peppered steak, play up the pepper with a punchy Californian Syrah or a big Australian Shiraz.

CASSEROLE

Lots of latitude: consider reds from the Rhône (like Crozes-Hermitage), or the Languedoc (like Saint-Chinian), Californian Syrah, or Australian Shiraz.

HAMBURGERS OR MEAT LOAF

The reds for roast beef in more modest form—so everyday Bordeaux or New World Cabernet-Merlot, Spanish Tempranillo, Côtes du Rhône, and so on.

SPAGHETTI BOLOGNESE OR LASAGNE

▶ SEE PASTA, PAGE 28.

CHILI CON CARNE

Stick with Shiraz, Malbec, or Zinfandel.

GOULASH

▶ SEE CHILI CON CARNE, ABOVE—Chilean Merlot works well too.

MEATBALLS

With the tomato sauce you can afford to choose quite a gutsy red.
▶ SEE PASTA, PAGE 28.

STIR-FRY OR TERIYAKI

The rich, ripe reds again—Syrah or Shiraz, Shiraz-Grenache blends, Zinfandel, or Primitivo.

VEAL

ROAST

Choose between full-flavored, off-dry whites (Austrian Grüner Veltliner, Alsace or North American Pinot Gris), and medium-bodied reds—Burgundy, Bordeaux, Chianti, New World Merlot.

ESCALOPES

IN BREADCRUMBS
▶ SEE COLD VEAL, ABOVE.

IN CREAM SAUCE
Pinot Gris, any dry Riesling, or a light Chardonnay.

BRAISED (OSSO BUCCO)

Medium to full-bodied whites: a ripe, fruity Vernaccia, Australian Semillon, or Californian Marsanne.

GAME AND OFFAL

Certain red wines have an earthy, gamey character which may make them a natural choice for game dishes. (Mature Burgundy, for instance.) But not always! Some recipes are better suited to white wine.

GAME

PHEASANT OR PARTRIDGE
ROAST OR CASSEROLED
It's a traditional partner for mature Burgundy or Bordeaux, Barolo or good Chianti—but best Californian, Australian, or New Zealand Pinot Noir also turns it into a treat.
WITH APPLES
Better with an off-dry white like Pinot Gris (Alsace or North American) or Australian Semillon.

QUAIL
▶ SEE ROAST PHEASANT, ABOVE.

PIGEON
▶ SEE ROAST PHEASANT, ABOVE.

RABBIT
Casseroled in cider or white wine, it may be best with a full-bodied white like Alsace Pinot Gris. If cooked in red wine, there's your answer: pick something gutsy like Cahors or Syrah/Shiraz. Otherwise, steer a middle course with Cabernet-Shiraz.
WITH MUSTARD
Chardonnay if you insist, but Pinot Noir or Merlot would be better.
WITH PRUNES
▶ SEE PORK, PAGE 43.

VENISON
Another excuse to produce some rich and ritzy bottles! We're talking full-throttle Italian reds like Barolo and Amarone; serious Rhônes like Hermitage; mature and classy New World Cabernet and Shiraz. Best budget solutions: Madiran or spicy Australian Mourvèdre.

OFFAL

LIVER
Almost any red will be fine: let the richness of the gravy help you to decide. The scale goes up in intensity: Beaujolais, Chianti, Navarra reds, southern Italians, Zinfandel, Syrah/Shiraz.

KIDNEYS
The earthiness of kidneys is perfectly echoed by Pinot Noir—especially from Burgundy.
KIDNEYS COOKED IN RED WINE
This needs something more robust, like Crozes-Hermitage or a meaty Syrah/Shiraz.

OXTAIL
Meaty reds, for sure— ▶ SEE KIDNEYS COOKED IN RED WINE, ABOVE, or consider Barolo, Brunello, Châteauneuf-du-Pape, Zinfandel.

PATES AND FOIE GRAS

CHICKEN LIVER PATE
Try a full-flavored white like Pinot Gris or a soft red like Pinot Noir (from the New World, especially).

ROUGH PORK TERRINE (PATE DE CAMPAGNE)
Beaujolais is particularly good with this. Next best: Loire reds like Saumur-Champigny or New World Cabernet Franc.

FOIE GRAS
This luxurious delicacy of duck or goose liver may be dogged by controversy—but not as far as wine's concerned. For once, there's wide agreement that sweet white wines do it most justice. Sauternes, Barsac, Hungary's glorious Tokaji Aszú, New World late-harvest Riesling… how can you resist?

CHEESE COURSE

Cheese and wine are widely regarded as a brilliant and versatile double act. Usually served after the main course, a selection of cheeses mops up any remaining red wine. But the awkward truth is that some cheeses go better with white or sweet wine than red, and some do wine no favors at all. Below, you'll find some partnerships that work. Why not serve a generous slab of just one cheese with a specially chosen bottle?

GOAT

As Sancerre and Crottin de Chavignol prove so sensationally, goat cheese and Sauvignon Blanc are a heavenly partnership. Loire wines go best with young cheeses; riper New World Sauvignons (from New Zealand, especially) suit more mature, pungent ones.

SHEEP

Consider countering the saltiness with a little sweetness. Italians enjoy Pecorino with Soave Recioto; demi-sec Vouvray and late-harvest Riesling also go well with many sheep's cheeses. But treat Manchego to a Rioja Gran Reserva or a majestic, mature Syrah/Shiraz.

SOFT

BRIE, CAMEMBERT, CHAUME
Young versions are flattered by light, fruity reds like Beaujolais Villages, Chinon or a simple young New World Merlot. Riper cheeses call for mature Bordeaux, Californian Cabernet, or Australian Cabernet-Shiraz.

HARD

CHEDDAR, GOUDA, EMMENTHAL, GRUYERE
Buttery, medium-bodied Chardonnay is a surprise star—from Burgundy, California, Western Australia, or New Zealand. Mature Bordeaux, Rhône or Spanish reds, Chianti Classico, and older Californian Sangioveses work, too.

PARMESAN
Nothing beats Amarone—unless, perhaps, a venerable Nebbiolo or Barolo!

PUNGENT

MUNSTER, MILLEENS, PONT L'EVEQUE
A difficult bunch. Münster is often eaten with Gewurztraminer, but you might be as well off with a gutsy southern French or southern Italian red, or a Californian Syrah.

BLUE

▸ SEE TRICKY FOODS, PAGE 10.

ROQUEFORT
The salt-and-sugar principle again: Roquefort shines with Bordeaux's glorious sweet wines, Sauternes and Barsac. Botrytis Semillon-Sauvignon is the New World equivalent.

STILTON
Stick to tradition with port – preferably tawny.

GORGONZOLA, DOLCELATTE
Amarone to amplify the Italian flavor—or late-bottled vintage or tawny port.

SOLVING THE MIXED CHEESE PLATE DILEMMA

If you want to serve a selection of cheeses, try to choose three or four which all go well with a particular style of wine. Wisest options for a totally mixed board are mature red wines, tawny ports and, believe it or not, best quality medium-to-full-bodied Chardonnays.

DESSERTS

An indulgent dessert with a wine to match makes a wonderfully hedonistic end to a meal. A treat which most of us allow ourselves all too seldom! Make sure that the wine is sweeter than the dessert, though, or your ambrosial liquid will taste horribly bitter.

FRUITY

APPLES

Tarts and pies are delicious with sweet Loire wines like Vouvray moelleux and Coteaux du Layon, German or Austrian Riesling Beerenauslese, and New World late-harvest Riesling. Caramelized Tarte Tatin goes well with richer Australian botrytis Semillon.

PEARS

For pear tarts, ▶ SEE APPLES, ABOVE. Pears poached in red wine suit sweet red wines like Rivesaltes and Banyuls from the south of France, or California Black Muscat.

LEMON

Echo the citrussy sweetness with a German or Austrian Riesling Beerenauslese or Trockenbeerenauslese, or a botrytis or late-harvest Riesling from the New World.

STRAWBERRIES, RASPBERRIES

Sauternes is the passport to heaven—but sweet whites from the Loire, Germany, or Austria, demi-sec champagne and semi-sweet New World sparkling wines are divine, too.

BLACKBERRIES

Try a young, sweet red from the south of France (like Rivesaltes or Maury), or California Black Muscat.

BLUEBERRIES

The flavor of these little berries is nicely off-set by a late-harvest Riesling.

GOOSEBERRIES, RHUBARB

These tart fruits both go well with German Riesling Beerenauslese or botrytis Riesling from the New World —but you'll get by with almost any light Muscat.

PEACHES, NECTARINES, MANGOES

Oh, what a choice! Sauternes or Barsac, German or Canadian Eiswein, German or Austrian Riesling Auslese, Australian late-harvest Riesling… but if the fruit is poached in red wine, you may prefer a sweet red.

APRICOTS

Pick up on the wonderful apricot flavors in Hungarian Tokaji Aszú, the sweet Loire whites of the Coteaux du Layon, or Australian botrytis Semillon.

ORANGES

California Orange Muscat is the obivous thing, but remember there are lovely hints of orange in Muscat de Beaumes de Venise, Portugal's Moscatel de Setúbal, Hungarian Tokaji, and many New World late-harvest Rieslings.

PLUMS

Sweet Rieslings slip down best—whether Californian or Australian and botrytised, or from Germany, Austria, or Alsace.

MOUSSES, PAVLOVAS, MERINGUES

Match their sweet, frothy nature with honeyed fizz like Moscato d'Asti from Italy, sparkling Vouvray, champagne doux, or any sweet North American sparkler.

CREAMY

ICE CREAMS
Not that easy. ▶ SEE TRICKY FOODS, PAGE 10. For fruit ices, ▶ SEE FRUITY DESSERTS, PAGE 52. Vanilla, caramel, coffee, and chocolate flavors go well with Muscats—especially Australian Liqueur Muscat and California Orange Muscat. Otherwise, have a glass of sweet fizz (▶ SEE MOUSSES, PAGE 52).

CREME BRULEE, CREME CARAMEL
Botrytis Semillon is a winner— whether Bordeaux-based (like Sauternes) or from Australia. You might equally enjoy sweet oloroso sherry.

PANNA COTTA
Choose something to suit the accompanying fruit (▶ SEE FRUITY DESSERTS, PAGE 52), or choose any sweet Muscat or botrysis Riesling.

CHEESECAKE
Sweet fizz is pleasantly refreshing (▶ SEE FRUIT FOOLS, PAGE 52) or try a late-harvest Riesling.

KEY LIME PIE
Amplify those tingling citrus flavors with a late-harvest or botrysis Riesling.

CHOCOLATE

WHITE AND MILK CHOCOLATE
Light chocolate suits light Muscats like Beaumes de Venise or St Jean de Minervois, or California Orange Muscat. Sparkling Muscats (like Moscato d'Asti) harmonize nicely, too.

DARK CHOCOLATE
Decadently rich chocolate desserts taste terrific with sweet red wines like Banyuls or Maury from the south of France, Black Muscat from California, or Mavrodaphne from Greece. Port (tawny or late-bottled vintage) also goes beautifully with bitter chocolate.

MOCHA
After five years or more in bottle, sweet southern French red wines like Banyuls and Maury develop wonderful mocha flavors. Amarone's sweet red cousin, Recioto della Valpolicella, often has hints of coffee and chocolate, too.

NUTTY, STICKY, OR OTHERWISE RICH

PECAN PIE, WALNUT TART
Nutty, toffeeish Australian Liqueur Muscat is just perfect— or try a glass of Malmsey, the sweetest madeira.

HAZELNUT CAKE
The toasty character of Vin Santo, Italy's amber dessert wine, gives it the edge; sweet oloroso sherry and madeira are also tasty.

BISCOTTI
The only thing to do with these toasty, nutty little Italian biscuits, is to dip them into a glass of Vin Santo.

STICKY TOFFEE PUDDING
Australian Liqueur Muscat is the closest wine comes to liquid toffee. Again, sweet oloroso sherry and Malmsey madeira are tempting alternatives.

BANANA TARTE TATIN
Sweeter and stickier than those made with other fruits, banana Tatin belongs with the richest, gooiest dessert wines. ▶ SEE STICKY TOFFEE PUDDING, ABOVE.

THE MOST FLEXIBLE FOOD WINES

Maybe you're planning a buffet meal with lots of different dishes. Or maybe you're ordering wine for a large group in a restaurant. Either way, you'll need to choose bottles that will blend in easily with a wide array of flavors. Here are ten wonderfully food-friendly wines:

WHITE

Chardonnay (unoaked)

Sauvignon Blanc

Pinot Blanc

Pinot Grigio

Australian Riesling

RED

Merlot

Côtes du Rhône

New World Pinot Noir

Spanish reds (Rioja, Navarra, Penedès)

Australian Shiraz

RESTAURANT SAFE BETS

The wines on the page opposite go with a wide array of dishes, so bear them in mind if you're in a restaurant that serves eclectic modern food. In speciality restaurants, look out for some of these versatile and affordable solutions:

CUISINE	WHITE	RED
FRENCH	Alsace Pinot Blanc, Mâcon-Villages	Saumur-Champigny, Minervois, Côtes du Rhône-Villages
ITALIAN	Soave Classico, Lugana	Chianti Classico, Salice Salentino
SPANISH	Rueda, Albariño	Navarra, Valdepeñas
MEXICAN	Chilean or Californian Sauvignon Blanc	Zinfandel, Petite Sirah
CHINESE	German or Australian Riesling, Pinot Blanc	Beaujolais, New World Pinot Noir
INDIAN	Semillon-Chardonnay, Marsanne	New World Merlot, Zinfandel
THAI	Sauvignon-Semillon, Pinot Blanc	Shiraz-Grenache, if you must have red!

TOP 20
SENSATIONAL MATCHES

Tapas with **manzanilla sherry**

Guacamole with
Chilean Sauvignon Blanc

Tapenade toasts with **dry rosé**

Onion tart with **Alsace Pinot Gris**

Oysters with **Chablis**

Panfried scallops with
Austrian Grüner Veltliner

Gravlax with **dry Vouvray**

Salmon in a spicy crust with **Californian,
Australian,** or **New Zealand Pinot Noir**

Chinese food with
New World sparkling wine

Chicken satay with **Australian Semillon**

Roast turkey with **Australian Shiraz**
(especially from McLaren Vale)

Roast lamb with **red Bordeaux**
or **Rioja**

Roast or grilled beef
with **Ribero del Duero**

Pheasant with **mature red Burgundy**

Venison with **Barolo**

Foie gras with **Sauternes**

Goat cheese with **Sauvignon Blanc**

Dark chocolate dessert with **Banyuls**

Apricot tart with **Hungarian Tokaji Aszú**

Pecan pie with **Australian Liqueur Muscat**

STARTING WITH THE WINE...

We're all familiar with the classics; Chardonnay and Sauvignon Blanc, Cabernet Sauvignon and Merlot, Burgundy and Bordeaux. Here are food ideas for some more unusual wines.

WHITE

ALBARINO Shrimp, fish, salads, roasted vegetables.

CHENIN BLANC (New World) spicy vegetable or chicken dishes.

COLOMBARD Light salads or appetisers, Thai food.

CONDRIEU Lobster, crab, pork roast with apples, pears, or peaches.

COTES DE GASCOGNE Salads, kormas, light chicken, or vegetable dishes.

FRASCATI Seafood, fried fish, pasta with vegetables.

FUME BLANC Spicy fish cakes, chicken korma, roast vegetables.

GAVI Fish, seafood, cold veal.

GEWURZTRAMINER Onion tart, Münster cheese, some smoked fish.

GRUNER VELTLINER Scallops, pork stir-fry, roast veal.

JURANCON SEC Roast chicken, ham with melon.

LUGANA Light pasta dishes, fennel, seafood.

MARSANNE Creamy curries, butternut squash risotto, chicken/pork stir-fry.

MUSCADET Shellfish, especially mussels, oysters.

ORVIETO Light pasta, pizza or risotto, fish, antipasti.

PINOT BLANC Omelets, vegetable dishes, light Chinese food, Thai green curry.

PINOT GRIGIO Pasta with herbs or cream sauce, fish, antipasti, vegetables.

PINOT GRIS Onion tart, roast pork, rabbit in white wine.

RIESLING (German) Chinese food, stir-fries, goose.

RIESLING (Alsace) Cheese dishes, quiche, Chinese seafood or chicken dishes.

RIESLING (New World) Fish, shellfish, salads, light Chinese food.

ROUSSANNE ▶ SEE MARSANNE.

RUEDA Fish, seafood, salads, egg dishes.

SAVENNIERES Asparagus, river fish.

SEMILLON Spicy Asian chicken or pork (especially satay), roast chicken, pork with apples.

SOAVE Fish, seafood, light pizza or pasta, salads.

VERDELHO Ceviche, crab cakes, roasted vegetables, spicy dishes.

VERDICCHIO Fish, pasta in cream sauce, vegetable dishes, risotto.

VERMENTINO Fish, salads, light pizza or pasta.

VERNACCIA Fried fish, fish pie, light pasta, chicken, veal.

VIOGNIER Crab, lobster, Chinese scallops, roasted bell peppers.

VOUVRAY (Dry) Gravadlax, goat cheese, scallops, pork with prunes.

RED

AMARONE Richest meat dishes, venison, Parmesan cheese.

BARBARESCO Roast meats, game, dishes with truffles.

BARBERA Pizza, pasta with tomato sauce, ham.

BAROLO Richest meats, game, mushroom and truffle dishes.

CAHORS Duck confit, cassoulet, rabbit in red wine.

CARMENERE Beef in all its forms.

CHIANTI ▶ SEE SANGIOVESE.

CHINON ▶ SEE BOURGUEIL.

CORBIERES Roast meats, gutsy meat casseroles, spicy sausages, liver.

CROZES-HERMITAGE Duck, roast pork, game, kidneys in red wine.

DOURO Wide range of meats, rich vegetable casseroles.

FAUGERES ▶ SEE CORBIERES.

FITOU ▶ SEE CORBIERES.

GAMAY Soft cheeses, cold meats, ham, pork, pork-based patés.

GARNACHA/GRENACHE Barbecued meats, spicy Asian beef dishes.

GIGONDAS Robust meat or game dishes, peppered steak.

MADIRAN Duck confit, meaty stews.

MALBEC Roast beef, beef stews, chili con carne.

MINERVOIS ▶ SEE CORBIERES.

MONTEPULCIANO D'ABRUZZO Pizza, pasta, wide range of meats.

MOURVEDRE Spicy or peppery meats, venison.

NEBBIOLO Rich meats, game, offal, mushroom dishes.

NEGROAMARO Pasta in rich sauce, robust meat dishes, liver.

NEMEA Moussaka, goulash, spicy meat dishes, lamb kebabs.

NERO D'AVOLA
▶ SEE NEGROAMARO.

PETITE SIRAH Mexican dishes with cheese, chicken, beef.

PINOTAGE Spare ribs, meats—char-grilled especially.

PINOT NOIR (New World) Pan-seared salmon, tuna, duck, Chinese meat dishes.

PRIMITIVO Spicy meat or vegetable dishes, spicy sausages, pasta with meat sauce.

PRIORATO Duck confit, rich meats.

RIBERA DEL DUERO Roast meats, mature cheeses.

RIOJA Lamb, game, roast chicken, pork, manchego cheese.

SAINT-CHINIAN ▶ SEE CORBIERES.

SAINT-JOSEPH
▶ SEE CROZES-HERMITAGE.

SALICE SALENTINO
▶ SEE NEGROAMARO.

SANGIOVESE Pasta with meat sauce, braised beef, steak, calves' liver.

SAUMUR-CHAMPIGNY
▶ SEE BOURGUEIL.

TEMPRANILLO Lamb in all forms, other meat, poultry.

VACQUEYRAS ▶ SEE GIGONDAS.

VALDEPENAS Mediterranean-type dishes with garlic, olives, herbs.

VALPOLICELLA Pizza, pasta, light meats.

ZINFANDEL Spicy Asian or Mexican meat dishes, sausages, pasta with meat sauce.

INDEX

PHOTOGRAPHY BY:

Alan Williams; back jacket 1, 4, 8, 10, 11, 17, 18-19, 21, 29, 34, 36, 44, 45, 51, 53, 56-57, 60-61.

Peter Cassidy; 2, 14, 20, 42-43, 47.

Debi Treloar; 24-25, 55, 58-59, Endpapers.

William Lingwood; front jacket, 9, 12, 26, 32-33.

Ian Wallace; 6, 35, 39, 41.

Francesca Yorke; 13, 48-49.

Martin Brigdale; 54

James Merrell; 3

William Shaw; 31

Philip Webb; 22

ACKNOWLEDGMENTS

First, special thanks to my Australian friend and culinary mentor, Kate Engel, who introduced me to the excitement of food and wine matching years ago at her Dublin dinner table. Discovering great flavor combinations has been a pleasurable obsession ever since. A big hug of gratitude is also due to Jonathan Ray for propelling me towards this project.

I would like to thank Alison Starling of Ryland Peters & Small, Inc. for her enthusiasm for the idea from the start; Miriam Hyslop for her sensitive editing, and Paul Tilby for his finely tuned aesthetics. Finally, I raise a glass (again!) to my terrific in-house tasting team: Bob, Simon, Victoria, and Mark.